Contents

How to use this book

Yellow boxes give you useful tips to help you understand the questions.

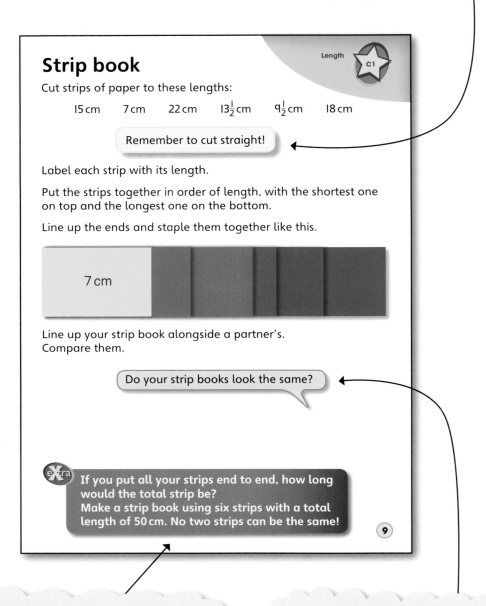

Strip book

Length C1

Cut strips of paper to these lengths:

15 cm   7 cm   22 cm $13\frac{1}{2}$ cm $9\frac{1}{2}$ cm   18 cm

Remember to cut straight!

Label each strip with its length.

Put the strips together in order of length, with the shortest one on top and the longest one on the bottom.

Line up the ends and staple them together like this.

7 cm

Line up your strip book alongside a partner's. Compare them.

Do your strip books look the same?

eXtra If you put all your strips end to end, how long would the total strip be?
Make a strip book using six strips with a total length of 50 cm. No two strips can be the same!

9

If you finish the main activity before the end of the lesson, you can move on to the Extra activity.

Speech bubbles raise interesting questions that you can discuss with others in your group.

2

Target 100

You will need these two dice:

How to play

Choose a start number between 25 and 40.

Roll the two dice to find out
how much to count on or back.

Now your partner does the same.

Keep taking turns, and write all the numbers in a list.

Start number.	2	6	
You add 1.	2	7	
Your partner adds 10.	3	7	
You take away 20.	1	7	
Your partner adds 1.	1	8	

Play the game.

Your target is 100. If you get to exactly 100, you win. If you go over 100, your partner wins.

Do you see any patterns in your list of numbers?

If you have time, play the game again.

 **What do you think of the game? How could you change it to make it better?
Try the game with your changes to see if they improve it.**

Moving the zero

Take any two digit cards.

Use them to make a 2-digit number.

For example:

3 and 5 ⟶ 3 5 or 5 3

Add a 0 card to make three 3-digit numbers.

For example:

3 5 ⟶ 0 3 5 , 3 0 5 and 3 5 0

> Is it possible to make any other 3-digit numbers in this way?

Write your three numbers.
Your teacher will underline one digit in each number.
Write the value of each underlined digit.

0	3	5	three tens, 30
3	0	5	three hundreds, 300
3	5	0	zero units, 0

Repeat, starting with two new digit cards.

 eXtra Take three digit cards. Find all the different 3-digit numbers that can be made. Write the numbers in order, from lowest to highest. What do you notice?

Digits

Choose three digits.

Use them to make as many different numbers as you can.
You can only use each digit once in any number.
You do not have to use all the digits in each number.

1 Write all the numbers that you find.

> How can you be sure you have found all the possible numbers?

2 Write the numbers in order from smallest to largest.

	1
	5
	7
1	5
1	7
5	1
5	7

> Does this make it easier to see whether you have found all the numbers?

 How many numbers did you make using your three digits? Do you think you could always make the same number of numbers using any three digits? Why?
Choose three different digits and test it out. Were you right?

Star numbers

1 For each star write the numbers in order from smallest to largest.

2 Draw a 0–100 number line. Remember to use a ruler! Put all the numbers in the right places on the line.

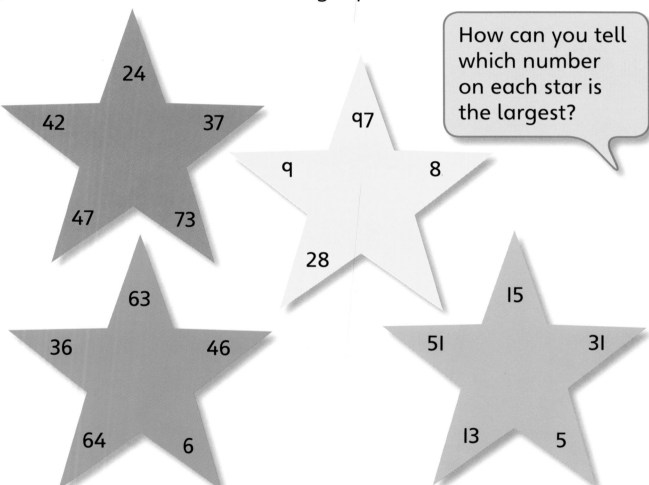

How can you tell which number on each star is the largest?

3 Using a different coloured pencil, add 10 more numbers to your number line.

 Draw a star. Write five numbers in it. Use any numbers up to 999. Ask a partner to write the numbers in order. Work together to place them on a 0–1000 number line.

Fame and fortune

Mr Moneybags and Miss Bigbank are celebrities. They are always arguing about who has more money.

On Monday, Mr Moneybags has £550 in his wallet. Miss Bigbank has £500 in her purse. During the week, they each get more money.

Monday	£550	£500
Tuesday	£19	£27
Wednesday	£25	
Thursday	£9	£44
Friday	£12	£47

1 How much do they have on each day?
   Use PCM 7 to help you to count on.

2 Who has the most money on Friday?

 Miss Bigbank wants to give £129 to charity, then decides to give an extra £25. Fill out her cheque on PCM 7.

Missing coins

Asha starts with 12p in her purse. But each time she looks in her purse there are some coins missing!

Asha only has 1p, 2p, and 5p coins.

| 1p | 2p | 5p |

Which coins are missing from Asha's purse?

For each picture, write which coins she needs, then write a number sentence to match.

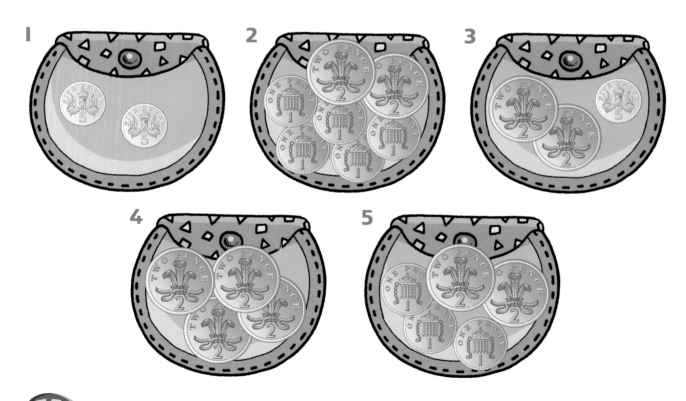

1

2

3

4

5

eXtra

Milek knows he has 27p in his money box. But he can't see inside it without breaking it. What coins might he have in there? Try to find all the possibilities.

Strip book

Cut strips of paper to these lengths:

15 cm   7 cm   22 cm $13\frac{1}{2}$ cm $9\frac{1}{2}$ cm   18 cm

Remember to cut straight!

Label each strip with its length.

Put the strips together in order of length, with the shortest one on top and the longest one on the bottom.

Line up the ends and staple them together like this.

7 cm

Line up your strip book alongside a partner's.
Compare them.

Do your strip books look the same?

 If you put all your strips end to end, how long would the total strip be?
Make a strip book using six strips with a total length of 50 cm. No two strips can be the same!

C1

Measure me!

Draw a picture of yourself. Add labels like the ones below.
Estimate your measurements and write your guesses.
Work with a partner to measure each other.
Fill in your measurements. Write 'cm' for centimetres,
and 'm' for metres.

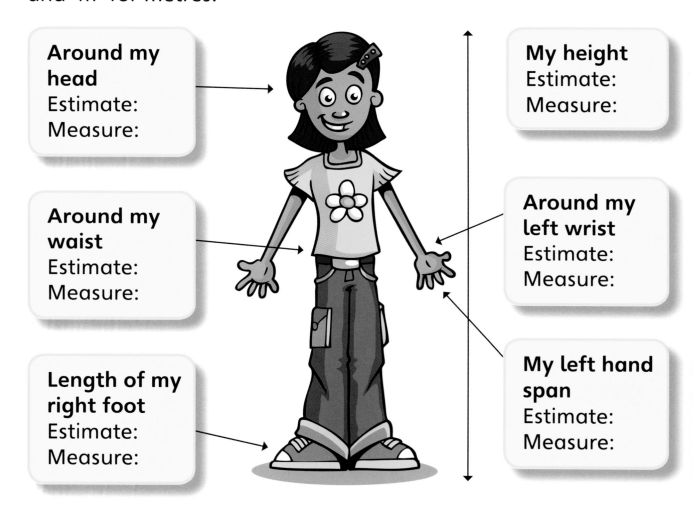

Around my head
Estimate:
Measure:

My height
Estimate:
Measure:

Around my waist
Estimate:
Measure:

Around my left wrist
Estimate:
Measure:

Length of my right foot
Estimate:
Measure:

My left hand span
Estimate:
Measure:

Compare your measurements with a partner. Does the shorter person have the smallest foot? Does the person with the larger hand span have the biggest wrist? Now compare your measurements with other children. Are the answers to the questions the same?

30 days hath September

> 30 days hath September,
> April, June and November.
> All the rest have 31, except February clear,
> Which has 28, or 29 in each leap year.

1 Write the months in order, starting from January.

2 Use the poem to help you work out how many days there are in each month. Write the number of days next to each month.

Use your list to help you answer these questions:

3 How many days are there in spring?

4 How many days in summer?

5 How many days in autumn?

6 How many days in winter?

How did you work it out?

Which of these answers would change in a leap year? Why?

eXtra Add the days in your birth month and the days in a partner's birth month. Find another partner and add the days in your birth month and the days in their birth month. How many different possible answers are there?

(11)

What's missing

These pictures are symmetrical.
Half of each picture has been cut off by mistake!

Copy the pictures and draw the missing half.

1
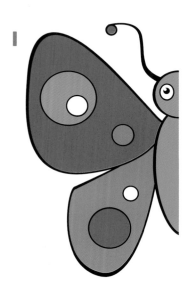

2

3

4

Fold a piece of paper in half. Draw half a picture on one side. Give the piece of paper to your partner. They complete the drawing. How can you check that they have drawn it correctly?

What is the shape?

Copy these 'upside-down' words and draw
their reflections.

I
bɐυｆɒɓou

2
µɐxɒɓou

3
ocｆɒɓou

4
ｇnɒbᴉɹɐｆɐᴉɐｆ

5   Draw a shape to match each word.

6   Draw a mirror line along one side of each shape
    Reflect each shape in the mirror line.

Have the shapes changed? How?

 Try some mirror writing. Write your name on a
piece of paper. Hold it up to a mirror. What does it
look like? Write your name so it looks correct when
you hold it up to the mirror. Can you think of any
uses for mirror writing?

Crocodile teeth

Baby Croc is losing his baby teeth!
Every time he eats a fish one of his teeth falls out.

Throw the dice and feed that number of fish to Baby Croc.

How many teeth are left?

> How will you work this out?
> How will you record what you've done?

Repeat until all his teeth have fallen out.

eX**tra** When Baby Croc bites a stick by mistake, 10 teeth fall out at once! If he eats 9 fish and bites 1 stick, how many teeth will he lose? Make up some questions like this for your partner.

Function machines

Choose a number card between 0 and 9.
Put it in the **start** box of this function machine.
Multiply it by 5 then double your answer.

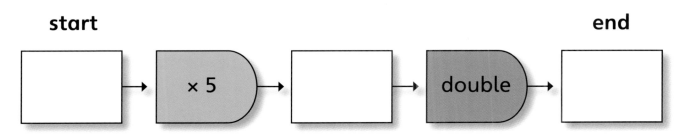

start   **end**

What number comes out in the end box?
How does the function machine work?

Copy and complete this table with your results.

Start	0	I								
× 5	0									
End	0									

Look at the start and end number in each example.
What do you notice? Describe any patterns.

 Make up your own function machines on PCM 23.
Put a number from 0 to 9 through each machine.
Try predicting the end numbers before you work
them out.

Which three toys?

key ring   pencil   top   balloon   paints   rubber   car

Each day Jenny went to the toy shop to buy three toys.
On Monday Jenny bought a key ring for 20p.

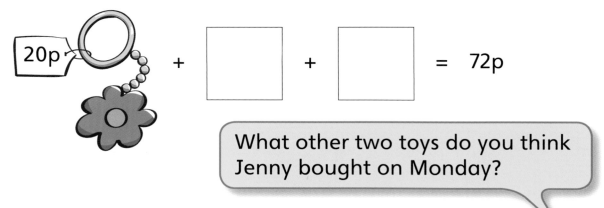

20p + ☐ + ☐ = 72p

What other two toys do you think Jenny bought on Monday?

1 On Tuesday Jenny spent 35p.
   Which three toys did she buy?

2 On Wednesday Jenny spent 80p.
   Which three toys did she buy?

3 On Thursday Jenny spent £1·60.
   Which three toys did she buy?

4 On Friday Jenny spent £2·07.
   Which three toys did she buy?

eXtra Choose four toys. Work out the total cost.
Write it on a piece of paper. Swap with a partner.
Can they work out which four toys you chose?
Which four toys did your partner choose?

Snack shop

THE SNACK SHOP

	Egg roll	35p
	Jam sandwich	25p
	Chicken wrap	50p
	Apple	15p
	Orange	12p
	Banana	19p
	Juice	40p
	Milkshake	55p
	Water	30p

Three friends, Amy, Bilal and Callie, visit the snack shop.

Amy buys a jam sandwich and an apple. She pays with a £1 coin. How much change will she get?

Think of a similar problem about the snack shop.
Write it on paper and work out the answer underneath.
Fold over the answer then swap with someone else.
Answer their problem. Compare your methods.

 extra

If you buy one sandwich, one piece of fruit and one drink, you get 20p off the total cost. Explore different combinations. How much change would you get from £1?

17

Odd and even dominoes

Look at the number of spots on each domino.
Sort your dominoes into three piles.

Pile I

| odd | odd |

Pile 2

| even | even |

Pile 3

| even | odd |

These two dominoes are the same!

| odd | even |

Look at one pile of dominoes at a time.
Turn each domino into an addition. Find the total.

| odd | odd |

5 + 5 = 10
1 + 3 =

| even | even |

2 + 2 = 4
2 + 4 =

| even | odd |

6 + 3 =
1 + 4 = 5

What do you notice about the totals in each column?
Which are odd? Which are even?

Are there any patterns?

Write and complete these number sentences at the bottom of the correct column:

odd + odd =   even + even =   even + odd =

eXtra Are the rules true for higher numbers?
How do you know?

Order puzzles

m	y	t	j	e	n
j	g	q	o	i	b
p	b	h	a	d	l
u	l	d	n	f	h
j	s	k	c	v	z
w	i	x	m	g	r

Find these letters:

- The third letter of the second row
- The fifth letter of the first row
- The sixth letter of the sixth row
- The first letter of the fourth row
- The second letter of the fifth row
- The fourth letter of the third row

Rearrange the letters and draw the mystery shape.

d	m	t	o	r	j
i	s	g	n	k	d
x	c	h	b	v	j
u	f	j	p	w	l
h	q	z	e	o	k
n	b	c	g	m	y

Find these letters:

- The third letter of the sixth row
- The fifth letter of the first row
- The sixth letter of the fourth row
- The first letter of the second row
- The second letter of the third row
- The fourth letter of the fifth row

Rearrange the letters and draw the mystery shape.

 eXtra

Make your own puzzle on squared paper. You will need to think about which word it could spell out, so that someone else could draw or write it. Give your puzzle to a partner to solve.

Greater than, less than

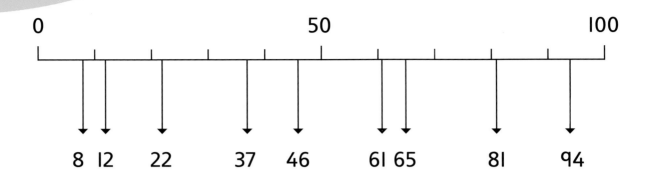

0   50   100

8 12   22   37   46   61 65   81   94

Use the number line to help you write 10 number sentences using > and <.

For example: 12 < 22

> How many of these number sentences could you write, using just nine numbers?

Write some number sentences using **two** of the > and < signs.

For example: 12 < 37 < 65
               12 < 37 > 22

> Do you have a rule to help you remember which sign to use?

Write some number sentences like this: 61 ☐ 94 ☐ 46.
Ask a partner to fill in the > and < signs.

 e**X**tra

Write some number sentences using these numbers:
247   163   391   452   319   425   274   136
Use two of the > and < signs in each sentence.

Square corners

Take two square pieces of paper – one blue and one white.

Fold the blue paper in half diagonally.
Cut it to make a right-angled triangle.

Place the blue triangle over the white square.

Cut out a right-angled triangle from the blue paper. Place it on the white paper like this.

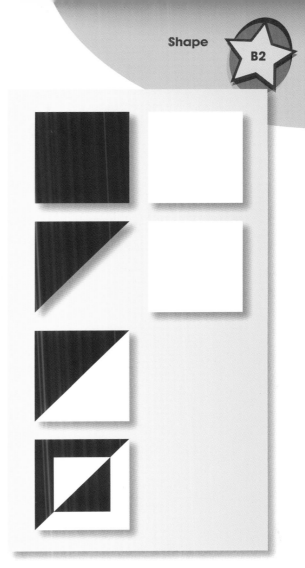

1   How many right angles are in your pattern?

2   How many of them are blue?

3   How many of them are white?

4   Are any of them blue and white?

5   Make your own designs using blue and white squares. How many right angles can you make?

Is your pattern symmetrical?

 Find right angles around the classroom or school. Use a digital camera to record what you find.

Ice-skating

Here are some jumps that ice-skaters make.

Some jumps turn all the way round, like this one.

This is a whole turn in the air.

Some jumps only turn half-way round, like this one.

How many right angles in a half turn?

Four skaters did a routine.

- Skater 1 did one whole turn anticlockwise, then skated on.
- Skater 2 did a $1\frac{1}{2}$ turn when she jumped on her skates.
- Skater 3 did two whole turns anticlockwise.
- Skater 4 did a whole turn in a clockwise direction.

Which of these diagrams belong to each skater?

a   b    c    d

eXtra

Make up your own skating routine using the cards on PCM 32. Record the routine using diagrams and words. Describe your routine to a partner.

Getting to the wedding

Mr Jordan is going to a wedding.
He needs to get from his house to the church.
There are several possible routes.

Describe one of the routes to a partner as if you were on the phone.

Your partner draws a diagram of the route as you describe it.

Did they draw it correctly?

Now it is your partner's turn.

 **Draw your route to school showing all the turns.
Describe it to your partner. Check it on a map.**

Tom's drinks

The chart shows the different types of drinks Tom had every day for a week.

	water	tea	apple juice	orange juice	cola	orange squash
Mon	3	1	0	1	1	2
Tue	3	0	1	0	0	4
Wed	4	0	1	0	0	3
Thu	3	2	0	1	0	2
Fri	4	1	1	0	0	2
Sat	2	2	2	0	2	0
Sun	1	4	0	1	1	1

Draw a block graph of Tom's drinks.
Use your graph to answer these questions.

1 How many orange drinks did Tom have in a week?

2 How many fizzy drinks did Tom have in a week?

3 Which drink did he have most of?

4 Which drink did he have least of?

5 How many hot drinks did Tom have in a week?

6 How many drinks did Tom have in a week?

Which drink do you think is Tom's favourite?

Take turns to ask each other questions about the data.
Answer them using the chart or the block graph.

Fun in the snow

After we had made a snowman, Mum collected all the wet clothes. She found:

11 soggy socks

8 wet gloves

7 snowy wellington boots

4 pairs of wet jeans

Draw a pictogram showing the clothes in pairs.

Use symbols like this:

one pair of socks   one pair of gloves   one pair of wellies   one pair of jeans

How could you show half a pair?

Use your pictogram to answer these questions.

1   How many people helped to make the snowman? How do you know?

2   Which items of clothing has Mum not found yet?

3   How many items of clothing is Mum going to put in the washing machine? Don't include the wellies!

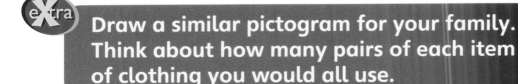

eXtra

Draw a similar pictogram for your family. Think about how many pairs of each item of clothing you would all use.

25

The shape sorter

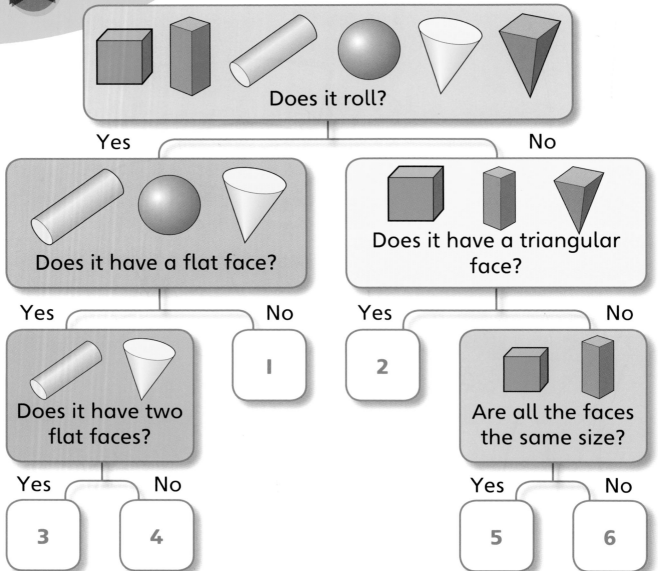

Draw the missing shapes and write their names.

How did you choose which shape went where?

Check your answers together.

How much change?

Tom and Isaac each have 20p to spend in the shop.

1 Tom buys a comic for 11p. How much change does he get?

2 Isaac buys a pencil for 9p. How much change does does he get?

Rafael and Shona each have 50p to spend in the shop.

3 Rafael buys a present for his mum. It costs 31p. How much change does he get?

4 Shona buys some crisps. They cost 29p. How much change does she get?

extra You have 50p to spend in the shop. Decide how to spend your money. Can you spend all of your money so that you have no change? How could you do it?

Exploring multiples

Count in 2s up to 50.

1 On PCM 42, draw a circle round each number in your count.

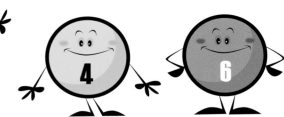

What patterns do you notice?

2 Predict some numbers that you would reach if you continued your count past 60.

Count in 5s up to 50.

3 On PCM 42, draw a square round each number in your count.

4 What patterns do you notice?

5 Predict some numbers that you would reach if you continued your count past 60.

6 Which numbers on the number square were in both of your counts?

What do you notice about these numbers?

eXtra
Count in 3s up to 50. On PCM 42, draw a line under each number in your count. Which numbers were also in your first two counts? What do you know about these numbers?

Known multiplication facts

£2   £4   £6

I   Copy and continue the sequence, counting up in £2s.

£20   £40   £60

2   Copy and continue the sequence, counting up in £20s.

Copy and complete these pairs of multiplication facts.

3   3 × £2 =

3 × £20 =

4   9 × £2 =

9 × £20 =

5   6 × £2 =

6 × £20 =

What do you notice?

6   Write some other linked pairs of facts from the 2 and 20 times-tables.

7   Can you write some other linked pairs of facts, using other times-tables?

Write a sequence counting on in steps of £5.
Write a sequence counting on in steps of £50.
Write some linked pairs of multiplication facts
for the 5 and 50 times-tables.

Plates of fruit

In a snack shop you pay for the fruit you put on your plate.

A grape
costs 2p.

A strawberry.
costs 5p.

A cherry
costs 10p.

Work out how much each plate of fruit costs.

Make up a plate of fruit for yourself.
How much does it cost?

eXtra Add another fruit, and give it a price. Draw some plates of fruit including your new fruit. Work out the total costs. Give your sheet to a partner and challenge them to work out the price of your new fruit, using the total costs.

Frog additions

Can you remember the number bonds to 10?

$1 + 9 = 10$

$5 + 5 = 10$

$2 + 8 = 10$

$3 + 7 = 10$

$4 + 6 = 10$

Freddy Frog uses number bonds to 10 to add.
He must make two jumps to find the answer.

- Freddy has this number sentence: $36 + 8 =$
- He adds 4 to get to 40. $36 + 4 = 40$
- Now he needs to add 4 more. $40 + 4 = 44$
- So the answer is: $36 + 8 = 44$

Use number bonds to 10 to complete these number sentences.
Use a 1–100 number line to help you.

1   $34 + 7 =$ 2 $56 + 8 =$ 3 $49 + 6 =$

4   $67 + 5 =$ 5 $88 + 6 =$ 6 $74 + 9 =$

7   $45 + 7 =$ 8 $58 + 8 =$

 eXtra

Write some number sentences where Freddy only needs to make one jump to find the answer. Show how you can find the answers using a number line.

Kangaroo additions

Why do number bonds to 10 make adding easier?

Kim Kangaroo uses number bonds to 10 to help her to add pairs of 2-digit numbers.
She makes three jumps to find the answer.

Kim has this number sentence: $57 + 17 =$
She adds 3 to get to 60. $57 + 3 = 60$
She adds 10 to get to 70. $60 + 10 = 70$
She needs to add 4 more. $70 + 4 = 74$
So the answer is: $57 + 17 = 74$

```
        +3      +10       +4
      ⌒      ⌒         ⌒
  ├────┬──┬─────────┬────┬──────────────┬─────────┬─────────┤
       57                74
 50                                                              100
```

Copy and complete these number sentences.
Use three jumps on the number line to help.

1 $29 + 19 =$ 2 $55 + 18 =$ 3 $18 + 16 =$

4 $72 + 19 =$ 5 $43 + 29 =$ 6 $63 + 28 =$

7 $27 + 26 =$ 8 $34 + 28 =$ 9 $46 + 39 =$

 eXtra   **What other method could you use to add the numbers above? Try out your method. Is it easier or harder?**

Queuing at the supermarket

Only one till in the supermarket is open.

The manager opens one more till and asks people to spread themselves equally between the two tills.

What happens to the number of people in each queue?

There are still long queues so the manager doubles the number of tills again.

1 How many people are in each queue now?

2 Draw a diagram to show what is happening.

3 Explain what happens to the size of the queue as the number of tills doubles.

One of the tills closes. The manager asks the shoppers in that queue to spread themselves evenly between the other tills. How many people are in each queue now?
Draw a diagram to show what is happening.

Matching outfits

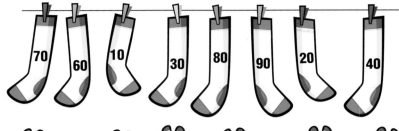

1   Match up the socks to make pairs that total 100.

2   Match up the gloves to make pairs that total 1000.

TROUSERS £30·00

JUMPER £20·00

VEST £5·00

SHIRT £15·00

3   If I spend £100, which clothes could I have bought? Write out a bill from the shop.

For example:

Item	Total
3 pair of trousers	£90·00
2 vests	£10·00
Total shopping bill	£100·00

How many options are there?

4   Write all the possible bills if I spend £100.

extra Write all the possible bills if I spend these amounts.
£50   £70   £75

Subtraction towers

$110 - 7 = 103$
$120 - 7 = 113$
$130 - 7 = 123$
$140 - 7 = 133$
$150 - 7 = 143$
$160 - 7 = 153$
$170 - 7 = 163$
$180 - 7 = 173$
$190 - 7 = 183$
$200 - 7 = 193$

Look at this subtraction tower.

The subtractions start on the ground floor and go all the way up to the roof.

Draw subtraction towers like this from these starting bricks.

1 $400 - 3$

2 $900 - 1$

3 $700 - 6$

Look at this subtraction tower.

How is it different from the first tower?

Draw subtraction towers like this from these starting bricks.

4 $600 - 2$

5 $500 - 9$

6 $800 - 7$

$390 - 4 = 386$
$380 - 4 = 376$
$370 - 4 = 366$
$360 - 4 = 356$
$350 - 4 = 346$
$340 - 4 = 336$
$330 - 4 = 326$
$320 - 4 = 316$
$310 - 4 = 306$
$300 - 4 = 296$

eXtra Draw six more subtraction towers using the starting bricks from questions 1–6. This time, use bricks 1–3 to make the second sort of tower, and use bricks 4–6 to make the first sort of tower. What do you notice?

Raffle ticket table

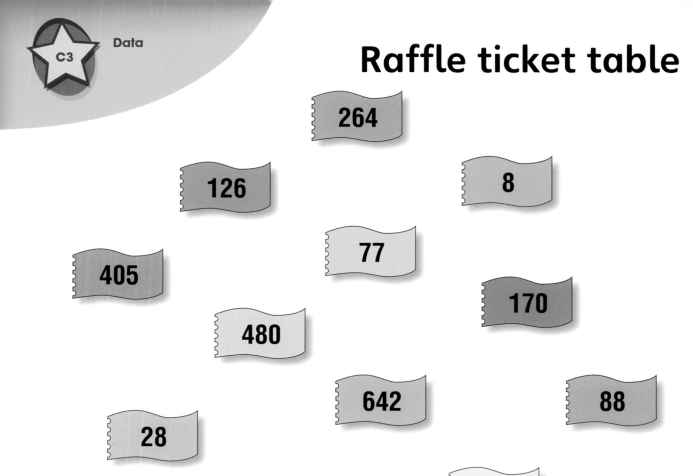

264

126

8

77

405

170

480

642

88

28

880

550

1   Complete the table of these raffle tickets on PCM 59.

Look at the number of ticks each ticket has.

2   Which ticket has the fewest ticks? Why?

3   Which ticket has the most ticks? Why?

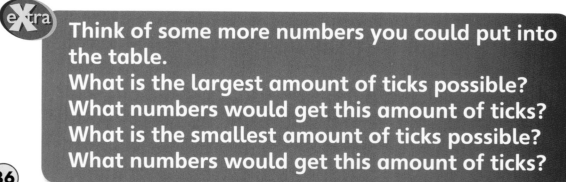

eXtra   Think of some more numbers you could put into the table.
What is the largest amount of ticks possible?
What numbers would get this amount of ticks?
What is the smallest amount of ticks possible?
What numbers would get this amount of ticks?

The cruise

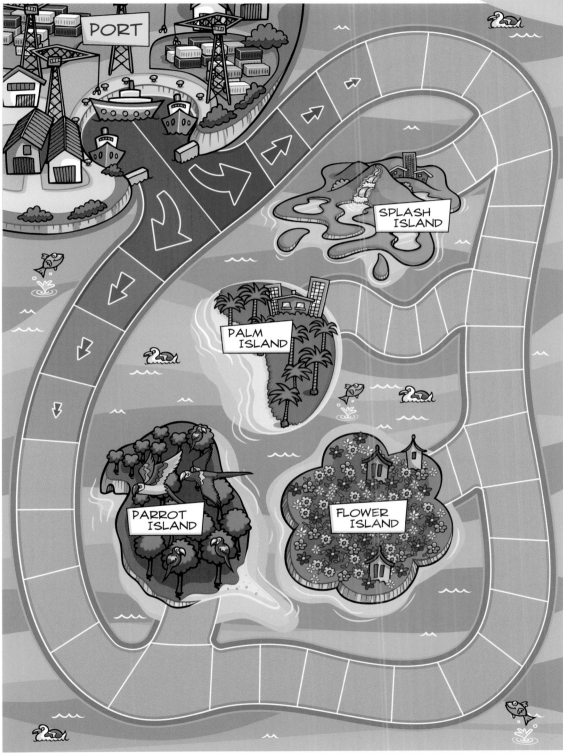

 What happens if the two cruise ships collide? Make up your own rules for what happens.

The clock shop

quarter past   o'clock

quarter to

quarter to

half past

half past

o'clock

quarter to

quarter past

Mr Wheeler owns a clock shop. He checks the time on each clock every morning when he opens his shop.

1 What do you notice about the time on the clocks?

Mr Wheeler goes on holiday. When he gets back he checks the clocks. They are all I hour late. He has forgotten to turn the clocks back for winter.

2 What time should all the clocks say?

3 Draw how an analogue clock would look at this time.

4 Draw how a digital clock would look at this time.

What patterns can you see?

 eXtra

There is a power cut and all the digital clocks stop working for 30 minutes. How slow are the clocks now?

Multiplying then dividing

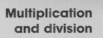

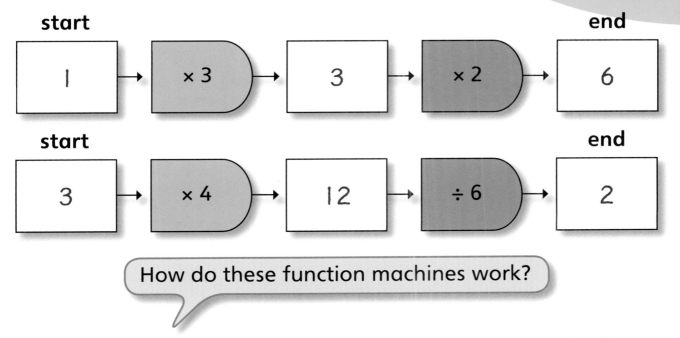

How do these function machines work?

The function machines on PCM 66 multiply then divide by the same number.

What do you think will happen to the numbers?

1 Choose a number between 6 and 9.
   Put it through the function machines on PCM 66.

2 Describe what happens when a number is put through these function machines.

3 Can you explain why this happens?

Use the blank function machines on PCM 66 to continue exploring what happens when you multiply then divide by the same number. Does it matter what number you start with? Does your rule always work?

Near doubles

Carlo and Anna are trying to find the answer to 34 + 35.
They decide to use doubling.

Carlo says

> Double the smaller number then add I.

> Is Carlo right?

Anna says

> Double the larger number then take away I.

> Is Anna right?

1 Find 34 + 35 using Carlo's method.

2 Find 34 + 35 using Anna's method.

3 Find 16 + 17 using Carlo's method.

4 Find 16 + 17 using Anna's method.

5 Whose method would you choose to work out 45 + 46? Why?

eXtra
Choose a method to work out these near doubles:
23 + 24 = ☐   18 + 19 = ☐
Compare methods with a partner.